Hold Up Jesus... How Do I Wait For MY HUSBAND?

Hold Up Jesus... How Do I Wait For MY HUSBAND?

ZION WILLIAMS

Hey Sis,

I know you have been out looking for your Boaz, but you have found this book instead. I am here to tell you, do not be discouraged! In fact, you are reading this because you are aligning with God's plan for your life. I know it is hard to wait in such an impatient culture where it seems like all the good men are getting snatched up a little too quickly. But Sis, let me keep it real... None of these men can compare to what God has planned for you. You are a prize, a queen, deserving, and loved. So let God give you what he has for **YOU**. If I can promise you anything, it is that God's promises are not going anywhere. Trust in His promise knowing *He has plans to prosper you and give you hope and a future* (Jeremiah 29:11). As my pastor always says, be encouraged!

With love, Zion

In loving memory of Papa, Henry George Williams. When you went to heaven, I realized I wasn't supposed to find the same love you had given me, but let your love live on by loving others the way you loved me. Kissy Hug

ONCE UPON A TIME NOT LONG AGO

♡

Easter Sunday 2023, I gave my life to Christ and got baptized. This was a trumpet moment in my life because I recently completed a lent fast that *dragged* me through the mud, but I made it through and devoted my life to Christ through repentance and water baptism. However, God wasn't done with me yet. I had more pruning to go through and one of my strongest vices? You guessed it...men!

After my lent fast God told me to fast from my relationship with men, but I was hesitant because I just came out of a 40 day fast and selfishly, did not want to fast again! But of course, God sent numerous confirmations, and one of them I received through my mentor who had given me a 40-day devotional and suggested that I read the book while '*maybe*' fasting from men. Whew. So, being obedient I read the devotional and took a leap of faith to cut off anything and everything that had to do with men. The first step was to unfollow several of them from social media, block who I needed to and make the decision to not entertain or come in contact with any male for the next 40 days. While I was undergoing the fast, I was journaling my thoughts and prayers for my future spouse and marriage.

During the fast God took it a step further and instructed me to write a book with my journal entries. He said that he would give me the divine ideas to write about, all I had to do was be the vessel and allow him to pour out through me. I leave you with a piece of me as everything in this devotional I have prayed for myself... As you embark on this journey, remember that you are not alone. Be encouraged, you have this book as a tool to guide you through your single season and be a blessing to your future marriage.

THIS ISN'T YOUR NORMAL DEVOTIONAL

♡

First, there are a couple of gems that I want to plant in your heart before you read this devotional.

GEM

Singleness is important because it teaches us how to be alone. Alone with God. So, practice being alone with God while you have the chance because, truthfully, that is how you will spend eternity.

GEM

I also want you to remember that as you say these prayers, God has already planted the desire of marriage in your heart. He has also spoken to you directly about being a wife, so keep in mind that when God speaks you must posture your heart in prayer and come in agreement to align with his will. Just because God said he will give you something it does not mean that you must sit back and say, "it will happen when it's supposed to." What you must do is say, "Lord, there is something that you have already purposed to do in the earth, and it also needs to be done in me. I need to come in full agreement in faith that indeed this is what you are about to do!"

Watch the Lord, wait until there is a word given to you by the Lord, then pray until what you are praying is seen.

GEM

Know that when you say the prayers in this devotional you are acknowledging that God has spoken a will into your life, and you believe him. Have the confidence to know that these prayers will allow God to give you strategy, wisdom, and understanding towards the promises he has given you.

How to Use this Devotional

Now, this devotional does require you to put some skin in the game, which means investing your own time and effort. This is a good type of investment, so you do not have to worry about your life crashing like how the stock market crashed. After reading the prayers there will be an "*Investment Account*" area designated for your "*stocks*" and "*bonds.*"

Stocks: Defined as putting a designated amount of money into a company and in return you receive a percentage of money back, a return on your investment. Because you invested into a company you are considered having "ownership." So, let us transition this to how you will invest in your "Spiritual Stocks." You make an investment by praying to God and because you have ownership over what you are praying for, He will give you a percentage back by answering the prayer. Which means you invested by praying and your financial return a.k.a "Spiritual Return" is God answering your prayers.

Bonds: Defined as putting a designated amount of money into a company but receiving your money back with interest. So, in the same way by investing in your "Spiritual Bonds" you give God a weakness so He can strengthen that weakness, and when he gives your "Spiritual Return" to you, you are now strengthened in that area of your life.

Example

Investment Account

Bonds:

Write down your answer to the verse and reflection question.

Stocks:

Write down your prayer that corresponds with the prayer of the day.

I also highly advise you to read the scripture associated with the investment account, from your own personal Bible, or the bible app on your phone so you can allow the Holy spirit to give you your own discernment and gain intimacy with your Father. Taking time to open your own bible and saying your own personal prayer allows God's spirit to move within you. Keep in mind when you do answer the questions it will expose those "bonds" a.k.a habits, character traits, thinking that you may need to let go off. As they are being revealed add them in your "stocks" a.k.a prayer and do not just ask God to take it away, ask him to replace it with a fruit of the spirit. For instance, I struggle with selfishness, I am aware of this trait, so I ask God to replace it with kindness. When you gain the knowledge about yourself, you also must pray for the wisdom to replace it with a Jesus- like quality.

This is an investment of a lifetime, **yourself**.

Table of Contents

Part I: Prayers for Before the Marriage

Part I: Prayers for When My Husband Comes

PART I

Prayers for Before the Marriage

ONE

TRUSTING GOD IN HIS TIMING

♡

The love story between Adam and Eve is beautiful. They did not have a traditional wedding or "save the date." Their marriage was divine and supernatural because they were already pre-destined to marry when God made Eve from Adam's rib. Let us quickly go through their love story. In the beginning God created the heavens and the earth....and then he made Adam! He made Adam so he could tend the earth and watch over it. God saw that Adam needed a mate, as well as desired one, so He created Eve from Adam, hence the word 'woman' came from. The rest is a bit "dragging" but let us focus on this piece. God made sure that everything was ready before bringing Adam on the earth and blessing him with Eve. God had to prepare where they would live, what they would eat and how they would survive. They also did not have to spend a "grip" on a wedding because God himself married them. All of this to say that God had his own timeline to make their marriage perfect in His eyes.

Yahweh, I trust that you are building my marriage before my husband and I even step into the union ship. You, Lord, must set everything in place for the marriage to be fruitful. Help me to have patience to wait for you to bring us together. I have complete confidence in knowing that I am tailor made for my husband in the same way Eve was tailor made for Adam, as she came straight from his rib. You are the overseer of my marriage because you set that structure in place when you married Adam and Eve. I lay down my own ideas, plans, and timing for my marriage to happen and allow your purpose to prevail in my love life.

In Jesus name, Amen

Investment Account

"Then the Lord God made a woman from the rib, and he brought her to the man. 'At last!' The man exclaimed."
Genesis 2:24 NLT

Read this verse and think about Adam's statement 'At last.' The meaning of *at last* is after much delay. Write down how having the heart posture of waiting will bring you in alignment with God and the marriage that He has planned for you. For me, having the heart posture of waiting allowed me to relinquish whatever control I thought I had in the decision of who my husband would be, how we would come together, and completely put that pressure on God because he will make it perfect in his timing.

Bonds:

____

____

Stocks:

____

____

TWO
ALLOW THE LORD TO GUIDE YOUR STEPS

♡

David is one of the most 'famous' persons in the Bible. He was a young shepherd boy when he defeated Goliath. He was later crowned King of Israel. David was praised for his reverence to God and was named by God - "a man after his own heart." What is evident in David's life is how the Lord ordered his steps. Let us imagine one of David's spoken word nights (writing a Psalms), when he expressed how safe and fulfilled, he felt by God. God was not only his shelter but his food and water as well, meaning he was not in need of anything because everything was provided by God. David spoke about how his heart, eyes, tongue, and body were focused on God. Most importantly he talks about how God lights up the pathway of his life and it makes it 100x easier *to follow the yellow brick road.* If I were an attendant at this spoken word night featuring David, I would be snapping my fingers away because that was beautiful! David's poem shows us how every part of his existence and being is fulfilled by God. If you give every part of your body and basic needs to God, there is no way he will not guide your path to your husband. Every aspect of your life will be so focused on God that your husband will walk into alignment as you are following the Lord's footprints.

PRAYER

Eli, I come to you asking that you guide my steps just as David allowed you to do for him. When trouble comes, I know to put my trust in you. My husband and I will hold on to the hope of the reward we gain when we get through our momentary troubles. In our marriage, we will think of whatever is pure, good, noble, and true. We pray against all devices of Satan before he even attacks. Lord, I ask you to take over my eyes, heart, body, and mind so I may focus on you and what pleases you. Let me be so entwined in who you are and how you have already fulfilled all my needs.

In Jesus name, Amen

Investment Account

"You make known to me the path of life."
Psalms 16:11

Read this verse and connect what areas of your life or yourself you need to focus on God more? Write down what ways you would want your future spouse to be more committed to God. For me, I need to focus my eyes more on God because I hear him, but I can take advantage of that and allow my eyes to be tempted by the other things in life.

Bonds:

____

____

____

____

Stocks:

____

____

____

____

THREE

BREAKING UP WITH THE OLD YOU

♡

As Paul was writing to the church of Ephesus, he stressed the importance of not living as the gentiles did. They knew the word of God but was ignorant to apply the word to their lives. Not only were they ignorant, but they were blatantly sinning and feeding their flesh. Paul reminds the church how important it is to "put off their old ways and be renewed in the Spirit of their minds so that they can walk in holiness and righteousness." As you are walking with God, he will strengthen you to break up with your old self and become the person he created you to be. As you become more like Christ, you will also become a better wife, one who will no longer carry childish or worldly ways.

Lord, today I pray that you help my husband and I understand the difference between a God centered relationship and a worldly one. In the past I operated with carnal mindset, depending on worldly relationships to bring me love and validation. I expected my old relationships to be the solution to my problems. I loved others out of fear and the effects of abandonment. All these things are wrapped up in a secular relationship, but when my husband and I put you first in our marriage, we know that there is a higher power that we must seek first before addressing issues and conflicts. Lord, help me to understand that sometimes all that I will be able to do as a wife is sit in the background and pray for my husband as he is trying to overcome a challenge. However, we will be diligent to pray and fast together as a couple to overcome things in our marriage. We understand that the love of God is what makes us whole. Lord, even if for a season I am receiving a lack of physical love from my husband, I know that I will be sustained by your everlasting love.

Help me to squeeze out and leave behind any worldly ideas that I had about relationships so you can teach me afresh and show me what a Godly marriage is supposed to consist of.

In Jesus Name, Amen

Investment Account

"You were taught, with regard to your former way of life, to put off your old self, which is being corrupted by its deceitful desires; to be made new in the attitude of your minds; and to put on the new self, created to be like God in true righteousness and holiness."
Ephesians 4:22-24

Read this verse and write down some old ways that you need to let go to fully be who God created you to be as a wife. For me, I can be very selfish and want to put my needs and wants first and expect other people to do the same for me.

Bonds:

____

____

____

Stocks:

____

____

____

FOUR

CONVERSION INTO THE NEW YOU

♡

Before Paul's conversion, he could not understand that Jesus was Lord, and since he could not grasp the understanding of our Savior, Jesus encountered Him while he was traveling to Damascus. The encounter left Paul blind for 3 days. In the sovereignty of his plan, God sent an apostle to heal Paul and his sight was restored. There was also a shift in his heart, and Paul now believed that Jesus is God's son, the one sent to die for our sins. Immediately after regaining his sight, Paul went back to Damascus and preached God's word with a supernatural understanding of who God is: *a message to let go of shame, guilt, fear, anything that you may have done wrong and start looking at yourself as God sees you, righteous, as the price of sin was paid by his son, Jesus.* I encourage you, as you are walking into a new calling such as a wife, mom, minister, pastor, etc. allow conversion of the heart to take place so you can fully function in that new role and see yourself as God sees you. As you embark on a new journey be assured that God trusts you with your new assignment. That is your license to walk confidently in that new calling.

Lord, I ask that I am constantly being made new by your Spirit before I even walk into a marriage. I completely surrender my life to you and allow you to create in me a pure heart and change me. As I am being purged, I will remember that you are doing it for my own good and you are making me a virtuous woman, equipping me for my calling and to build your kingdom. Lord, I ask when I do get married and start my life with my husband that I remember to maintain my identity in you. I am a child of God and when I am blessed with the title of "mother' and "wife," I will not feel as if I am losing a part of myself or losing a part of my freedom. Help me to understand that I am reaping the rewards and blessings that you promised me. I am building my own inheritance through God's grace and power.

In Jesus name, Amen

Investment Account

"Saul spent several days with the disciples in Damascus. At once he began to preach in the synagogues that Jesus is the Son of God.

Acts 9: 19-20

Read this verse and connect how being made a new creation through conversion allows you to walk with confidence in any title that God will give you. For me, it allows me to let go of any fear of not being a "good wife" or a "good mother" in the future.

Bonds:

Stocks:

FIVE

CREATING COVENANT

God, the creator of heaven and earth sent his only son, Jesus, who grew up in this world as any other human. Jesus was baptized in water by John the Baptist and later suffered a horrible death when he was crucified. When he was resurrected, some time had passed and then the disciples received the Holy Spirit. This is a wonderful example of an unshakeable covenant between the Trinity, "the Father, the Son, and the Holy Spirit," three Gods in one. Their plan of redemption is evident through a covenant relationship, that each member of the Godhead would fulfill their role so we can regain fellowship with our Maker. The trinity is the image of an everlasting covenant. God promised to send Jesus, then Jesus promised to send the Holy spirit.

Lord, I pray for an everlasting covenant in my marriage. A covenant between my husband and I with you, Lord, holding us together. Just as the trinity is God the Father, Jesus, and the Holy Spirit, so will my marriage represent love and oneness. Lord, let my husband love me as much as Jesus loves his bride, the church. Let there be love and respect in our marriage. Even when we do not feel like there is love for a season of our relationship, I pray that we will still have each other's best interest in mind. Lord, we must give sacrificially, passionately, and sincerely even when we do not feel like it because that is what love is. Father, I pray that our covenant helps to build each other's purpose in you. We build this covenant on the firm foundation of your truth.

In Jesus name, Amen

Investment Account

"For there are three that bear witness in heaven: the Father, the Word, and the Holy Spirit: and these three are one."
1 John 5: 7

Read this verse and connect how the oneness and love demonstrated in the Trinity can strengthen your relationship with your future husband. For me, I know that honoring a covenant is important, so it propels me to build a covenant with God so that I will have a strong covenant with my future husband.

Bonds:

____

____

____

____

Stocks:

____

____

____

____

SIX

BURDENS AND BLESSINGS

♡

In the book of Genesis, Jacob was enroute to find the house of Laban, his uncle. Let me give you a backdrop. Jacob was given strict orders by his father, Isaac not to marry a Canaanite woman, but go the house of his mother's father and find a wife there. While in route to the house of Laban, Jacob met Rachel, Laban's younger daughter. After working for Laban for one month, he asked Jacob about compensation for his service. Immediately Jacob asked Laban to marry his daughter, Rachel, because he had fallen in love with her. *"I will work for you for seven years in exchange for her."* Laban agreed! So, Jacob worked for seven years, and the years passed by quickly because of his love for Rachel.

After Jacob's seven years of service ended, he was to marry Rachel as agreed. However, Laban tricked Jacob on his wedding night and gave him his other daughter

Leah. *Gasp, the tea!* After coming together with Leah, Jacob realized the following morning that he was deceived. He went to Laban and said um, "you deceived me, that wasn't Rachel, the woman I love. Laban responded, "well by law you cannot have the younger daughter (Rachel) before the older daughter (Leah) is taken into marriage AND if you want Rachel, you must work an additional seven years for her. But Jacob did it without complaint because he loved Rachel, he is a true soldier because *sheesh, to* wait fourteen years for the woman you love is no easy feat. There are times when your blessing may come with a burden. However, it is your responsibility to steward the burden correctly to further maintain the blessing.

Heavenly Father, I pray that you prepare me for marriage and for the burdens that may come my way. Lord, I know that I am still responsible to steward the test and trials in my marriage, so help me to steward them just as equally as the blessing of the marriage. I pray that I will not fear the challenges in my marriage because I know that whatever I may go through will not break me because of your grace. God, you have already given me the blessing. You have already spoken it into existence, so help me to remain steadfast and focused on you so I can see it through any difficult circumstance. I ask you for a sustained marriage AND the tools to overcome burdens.

In Jesus name, Amen

"And Jacob did so. He finished the week with Leah, and then Laban gave him his daughter Rachel to be his wife."
Genesis 29:28

Read this scripture and connect how you can have an attitude like Jacob when it comes to waiting on God in faith and remaining steadfast until you receive the promise. For me, I can have a preserving mindset knowing there is success within the burden. I will continue in the burden of waiting for my husband, so I can finally receive the blessing of marriage.

Bonds:

____

____

____

____

Stocks:

____

____

____

SEVEN

FORGIVE

♡

This chapter may be scary for you, but it will bless you. Why will it bless you? That is because a pivotal aspect of our growth and maturity in Christ is based on forgiveness. The reason Jesus died on the cross is for us to be forgiven for our sins. God requires a heart of repentance and a heart that quickly forgives. Forgiveness is crucial in your walk with Christ because as he forgive you of your sins, so must you forgive others. To forgive others you must be intentional to release all offenses. You must forgive the people in your past, at your job, your parents, and most importantly your spouse, when you get married. You and your spouse will not be perfect, so learn *now* to forgive quickly. Forgiveness will strengthen your marriage and it will flourish when you do not allow a fault to stay in your heart for too long. Today's prayer is directly from Matthew 6:9-13, I'm sure many of you are familiar with this passage of scripture, but it is necessary to anchor your life in this foundational truth.

Our Beloved Father, dwelling in the heavenly realms, may the glory of your name be the center in which our lives turn. Manifest your kingdom realm and cause your every purpose to be fulfilled on earth, just as it is in heaven. We acknowledge you as our provider of all we need each day. Forgive us the wrongs we have done as we ourselves release forgiveness to those who have wronged us. Rescue us every time we face tribulation and set us free from evil. For you are the king who rules with power and glory forever. (Matthew 6:9-13 TPT)

In Jesus name, Amen

Investment Account

"And when you pray, make sure you forgive the faults of others so that your Father in heaven will also forgive you. But if you withhold forgiveness from others, your father withholds forgiveness from you."
Matthew 6:14-15

Read this prayer and think about those that you need to forgive. What has been weighing on your heart that God has been wanting you to let go off so he can fully heal you and restore you? How can you ensure you and your future husband are always in a place of not only forgiveness but learning more about yourself and each other when you forgive.

Bonds:

____

____

____

Stocks:

____

____

____

EIGHT

A WOMAN OF WISDOM

♡

Deborah is a woman not talked about much because of her small contribution in scripture. However, this woman was a powerhouse. She was the first woman to become a judge official, and she was a wife and a prophet. Although Deborah wore many hats she was always led by the Lord. During a war she told the Commander of the Lord's plans to help their army succeed. The commander listened but refused to go to war without Deborah being present. She replied, *"certainly I will go with you - because of the course you are taking the honor will not be yours, for the Lord will deliver Sisera into the hands of a woman."* Firstly, for a commander to want to take a woman with him to war was such an honor and shows how much Deborah was respected. Secondly, Deborah had to walk closely with the Holy Spirit to prophesy to the commander regarding going to war and the war's outcome. In the end they won the war, and just as Deborah said, a woman received the honor for the victory of the war. Deborah's wisdom and courageousness brought victory to the nation. Understand that many remarkable things can happen when you are a woman of wisdom.

Lord, I pray that I become a woman of great wisdom. I pray, Lord, that you will prepare and equip me to be the wife my husband needs. Help me to love him and be there for him every time he is in need. Keep my eyes and ears open to his feelings and needs in the relationship. Help me to be a role model for our children. Help me to love his family and not be selfish or insecure. Help me to love my husband in pure, honest, joyful love. Help me to honor my husband as we exercise faith in you. Help me to never idolize my husband, children, money, life, or myself. At the end of the day, I cannot be a good wife, mother, or woman without your divine wisdom.

In Jesus name, Amen

Investment Account

""Certainly I will go with you," said Deborah. "But because of the course you are taking, the honor will not be yours, for the Lord will deliver Sisera into the hands of a woman." So Deborah went with Barak to Kedesh."
Judges 4:9

Read this verse and connect how being a woman who walks in wisdom can amplify your relationships with your husband, kids, money, career, family, etc.

Bonds:

____

____

____

____

____

Stocks:

____

____

____

____

____

NINE
SECURED

♡

My girl Sarah was secured in her man Abraham! God also told Abraham that his family line would birth kings. Hard to believe when there were no mini-Abraham and Sarah's running around. Sarah was unable to have children for most of her life until one day God confirmed his promise by telling them both in *Mariah Carey's 'all I want for Christmas' voice*, "IT's TIMEEEE." The Lord said, "this time next year Sarah, you will have a child." Unfortunately, they did not believe God because both Sarah and Abraham were old and according to science you cannot have children at that age. It is important to note Abraham did have a son named Ishmael, BUT the mother was Sarah's servant, not Sarah herself. Abraham did not cheat, but Sarah did tell him to sleep with the servant because she was anxious for a child and thought that the promise God made them would come to pass through their maid servant. As promised, God came through and blessed

Sarah with a child. The lesson here is that Abraham stayed with Sarah even when she was not bearing children. Because of his relationship with God, he was blessed tenfold. Abraham held Sarah down and allowed her to be secured in him because he was secured in God.

PRAYER

Abba, Today I pray that on my darkest days and loneliest nights I have a husband that can guide me back to you because he is led by you. I pray that my husband is my confidant and knows how to nurture my anger, sadness, and disappointment. I pray that I will remember that you fill my heart up and not to place unrealistic expectations on my husband. He is not God, you are God. You are the great I AM, Jehovah Jireh, our Comforter. Being secure is feeling safe and protected, and protection and safety are found in you. I will always come to you to get my heart filled.

In Jesus name, Amen

Investment Account

"For I have chosen him, so that he will direct his children and his household after him to keep the way of the Lord by doing what is right and just, so that the Lord will bring about for Abraham what he has promised him."
 Genesis 18:19

Read this Verse and Connect how knowing your husband follows the Lord in all his ways, makes you feel more secure in your marriage. For me, it brings trust and comfort knowing my husband follows the Lord and has me and our family's best interest in mind.

Bonds:

____
____
____
____

Stocks:

____
____
____

TEN

IDOLIZING MARRIAGE

♡

I'm confident that you have heard about the 10 commandments at least once in your life. If you have been walking with Christ for a long time, then I am super confident that you know the FIRST commandment, *"thou shall not have no other Gods before me."* I mean reading that and knowing who God is, it feels like common sense to not have or want another God before him. But think about the importance of this being the very first commandment, it was not other commandments such as *do not kill* (which is still a commandment), but do not have any other Gods before me. This law is so important that the Devil tried to tempt Jesus to worship him before his own Father.

A quick synopsis of that story is after Jesus got baptized and was filled with the Holy spirit, he was led in the wilderness for 40 days and 40 nights to be tempted by the devil. While isolated and hungry Satan pulled every trick out of his magic hat to try and tempt Jesus. He told Jesus to turn a rock into bread, promised to give him authority over kingdoms if he worshipped him, and even to jump off a cliff to see if God would really save him. I do not know about anyone else but if I were Jesus I would be thinking about some hot, buttery, church's chicken biscuits. Safe to say I am not Jesus and his strength to say no after he was weary and beaten down for more than a month is commendable.

With that knowledge it is important to be mindful of the ways Satan can take what he knows God has already promised us and pervert it so we can worship that promise instead of God. Even if you do not worship the devil directly, it is still wrong to worship your future marriage. The devil knows how to distract you to put the want for marriage over your commitment to God. So, outsmart the devil by completely being committed to God and know in your spirit your marriage is coming in the right time.

Jesus, I come to you asking for the same power and strength you possessed when saying no to the enemy. That Satan attacks and tempts us when we are weak, but he is unaware that our spirit is strong. Help me to understand that I cannot fight without your power. I need your helping hand and I know anything I need is supplied by you Lord. Just as Jesus was confident in who God was, help me to have the same confidence. God help me deny my flesh daily and carry my cross just as Jesus did. I want to be more in my word and more intimate with you, so I know when is trying to distract me. Reveal whatever I may be putting in place of you. You are my number one, you are Alpha and Omega, and I serve and worship you alone.

In Jesus name, Amen

Investment Account

"Jesus replied, "The Scriptures say, 'You must worship the Lord your God and serve only him."
Luke 4:8 NLT

Read this verse and really think about if you are putting the promise of marriage before God. Write down how you can come back to being fully committed and serve only God. For me, when I was putting the promise before God, I asked him why I am not married yet and he said because 'I am not ready, and I love the idea of marriage more than I love him.' So, I went back and denied my flesh of everything I wanted other than God and allowed myself to be focused on my purpose in the now.

Bonds:

____

____

____

Stocks:

____

____

____

____

ELEVEN

PYTHON SPIRIT

♡

Okay sis let us have "the talk." I could not talk about marriage without bringing up this topic. I want you to be informed and have knowledge, so you are not taken advantage of. So, I leave you with tools and guidance as we talk about the story in Acts about Paul, Silas, and the python spirit. Paul and Silas were going to the temple when a fortune teller followed them shouting, *'these men are servants of the Most high God, who are you telling you the way to be saved."* This woman followed them for a few days shouting the same thing. Paul got fed up with her and said *"In the name of Jesus Christ I command you to come out of her! At that moment, the spirit left her."* Now this is important because we know that the devil is the father of lies. What the fortune teller said was true, but she was not speaking on behalf of the spirit of God, she was speaking under the influence of a python or fortune telling spirit.

Satan knows that God is bringing you a husband, so he is going to do everything in his power to keep you from that purpose. Satan will give you false hope, incorrect information, and a counterfeit. Again, you know that God said he is bringing you a husband so, when prophetic words are being said to you or words and situations are put in front of you - it may seem like it is from God when in fact it is from the enemy. Hear me when I say this, take everything back to God in prayer and as soon as he says that is not of him... Rebuke it! If you have the Holy Spirit within you then you have the power to rebuke the enemy in the name of Jesus! Do not be afraid. Be aware, watch, always walk and be submissive to the Holy Spirit.

PRAYER

El Shaddai, I ask that you to rebuke any spirit of python that may influence me, wanting to prey on the promises you have given me and turn them wicked. I understand that the spirit of python wants to disguise itself as a powerful mirage, it may speak truth, but it is not of God. This spirit may whisper lies about my future that never came from you Lord. It provides false hope and distraction, so I never put my flesh under subjection and seek your righteousness and truth. I rebuke this spirit if it is influencing me or lingering in other people in my circle. Increase my spirit of discernment and allow me to always be in your word so I can protect myself. Plaster a hedge of protection around me so that *my enemies may come at me from one direction but flee from me in seven.* No weapon formed against me shall prosper.

In JESUS name, Amen

Investment Account

"She kept this up for many days. Finally, Paul became so annoyed that he turned around and said to the spirit, 'In the name of Jesus Christ I command you to come out of her! At that moment the spirit left her."
Act 16:18

Read this verse, sit with the Holy spirit, and ask God if this spirit is upon you. Ask God to reveal anything you may be believing that he himself never gave you and write it down. Write down your own prayer and ask God to show you if there is anything that you need to let go of.

Bonds:

____

____

____

Stocks:

____

____

____

____

Part II

Prayers when your Husband comes.

TWELVE

BOAZ FINDS YOU, NOT THE OTHER WAY AROUND

Ahh, finally the moment that you have been waiting for... Boaz finally finding you! In the beginning I mentioned that you were probably looking for your Boaz, but you found this book instead. *Newsflash,* Ruth was not looking for Boaz either. In fact, Ruth was gleaning the field for herself and her mother-in-law, Naomi, when Boaz noticed her. It is important to highlight the qualities Ruth exemplified before being seen by Boaz. First, when Naomi lost her husband and sons, she left town and Ruth followed behind her even though there was a chance of never being remarried. Ruth was committed to taking care of Naomi and serving the same God she served. Ruth was hardworking because as went out to the hot field and picked up as much grain for herself and Naomi. In addition, she was loyal, selfless, and grateful. The qualities that Ruth portrayed are important because like Ruth, your "Boaz" will not find you without having certain character traits.

Ruth was stewarding the task God had already given her and maintained the attributes of a godly woman to gain the attention of Boaz. My encouragement? Focus on what is already in front of you, so when Boaz comes to pursue you, you are ready.

Lord, I come to you acknowledging that you are the creator of all things and ask that you specifically create my love story. I ask you to renew my mind and heart to be focused on you and that I live a life that glorifies and honors you. I pray for the attributes of a godly woman, and I pray that you do not allow my husband to come until you have completely refined me. When I have been refined by you and it is time for my husband to pursue me, I pray that he will yield to your voice and follow your instructions. I thank you that my husband will be ready for a wife and marriage and that he will honor and respect me. I thank you that when my husband comes, he will be filled with the Holy spirit and be led by you.

In Jesus name, Amen

Investment Account

"Boaz replied, 'I've been told all about what you have done for your mother-in-law since the death of your husband - how left your father and mother and your homeland and came to live with a people you did not know before."
Ruth 2:11

Read this verse and write down your qualities that God would want to cultivate within you, those same qualities that will "catch the attention" of your husband when he finds you. For me, God has cultivated loyalty, generosity, and a servant's heart.

Bonds:

____

____

____

____

Stocks:

____

____

____

____

THIRTEEN
PURPOSE IN MARRIAGE

♡

Joseph, Jesus' earthly father was disappointed and confused when he first found out that Mary was pregnant. She was a virgin, so it was impossible. Let me be real, he didn't get "none," but somehow, she was pregnant. Make it make sense! Let me lay it out for you! Mary was impregnated by the Holy Spirit, but Joseph was not aware of the Lord's plans. An angel had to visit Joseph to let him know (*in my own words*) "hey Joseph you to have to step up because we can't have the Messiah being born without a father." It was then that Joseph surrendered to the Lord's plan. I say all this to show how Mary's purpose of giving birth to Jesus, and Joseph's purpose of raising Jesus with Mary aligned with God's divine plan to eventually save humanity. The Holy spirit played a big part in Mary & Joseph's relationship because their union served a bigger purpose for God's kingdom. God has the same intentions for your marriage, to be of greater service than you, to build his kingdom, ensuring his purpose is fulfilled in your life.

Father, I pray that husband fulfills and guides my purpose, and I can fulfill and guide his purpose as well. I pray you protect me and my husband's calling from any weapon or snares of the enemy. I pray that the Holy Spirit moves within our relationship. I ask you that we will know our kingdom assignment and the purpose of our marriage. We will honor you and we thank you that our marriage will fulfill its commission on earth. We will serve you first in all things. Our marriage will build up your kingdom.

In Jesus name, Amen

Investment Account

"All this took place to fulfill what the Lord has said through the prophet:"
Matthew 1:22

Read this verse and write down the purpose God has entrusted you with to build his kingdom. (Write it down so when your husband comes you will be able to connect with the Holy Spirit to ensure you and your husband's purpose is in alignment with God's will).

Bonds:

____

____

____

____

Stocks:

____

____

____

____

FOURTEEN

THE APPLE OF HIS EYE

♡

Now, let us talk about Queen Esther. I do not want to sexualize Queen E. in any way, but the way she upheld herself is admirable, so that is what we are going to focus on and learn from. Queen Esther was treated like the *"Hilton sisters"* when she walked into the King's Palace. The King made a decree that he needed a new wife and Esther among other women adhered to beauty treatments and received the best of care for 12 months, so they could be presented before the King! *Forget Boaz, I want a King Xerxes.* Just kidding. After the beauty treatments, King Xerxes summoned Esther by name. She was chosen by the King because of her exceptional beauty. There is an important lesson in all this. It is important to realize how Esther and the other women went through the process of beautifying themselves before coming into the presence of the King. As you are waiting on your husband take note that your physical appearance is just as important as your spirituality.

Adonai, I thank you that I am fearfully and wonderfully made. As I groom myself in preparation for marriage, I pray that I am not only presentable but admired. I do not want to be admired in a vain way, but in a way that complements my inner beauty. When my husband and I have been married for many years, I pray that I will still find the desire to maintain my physical appearance and stay in shape. I pray that he too finds the importance of grooming himself as well as the importance of exercising regularly. Let my husband appreciate me for who I am, as I appreciate him for who he is. I pray that our love, respect, and admiration for each other will never end.

In Jesus name, Amen

Investment Account

"She pleased him and won his favor. Immediately he provided her with beauty treatments and special food. He assigned to her seven female attendants selected from the kings palace and moved her and her attendants into the best place in the harem."
Esther 2:9

Read this verse and connect how having the knowledge of who God is makes you want to cherish your body more and engage in self-care. Also, how do you expect your husband to groom and carry himself?

Bonds:

____

____

____

____

Stocks:

____

____

____

____

____

FIFTEEN

DEFEATING TEMPTATION

Let us talk about the story of Joseph and Potiphar's wife in the book of Genesis. Joseph, a man of honor, was serving a Captain of the Guard, Potiphar, in his home. His wife, 'miss thang' had a thing for Joseph and began to make sexual advances towards him. The scriptures described Joseph as well-built and handsome, and his appearance captured the heart of Potiphar's wife. She wanted Joseph BAD; and she would try to get him to come to bed with her. Joseph knew that it was wrong and told her, "No" every time she tried to make an advance. *Miss thang* tried once more to get Joseph to commit adultery but as he was running from her and the temptation to sin, he left his robe behind. Potiphar's wife, being embarrassed, decided that she would tell her husband that Joseph tried to sleep with her, using his robe as evidence.

I am sure that it was not easy for Joseph to turn down a beautiful woman, considering he was single and a virgin. However, Joseph was a man of character, he knew the influence of his position, and he respected his master and God's commandments. Although he was falsely imprisoned, Joseph defeated the temptation of sexual sin because he knew committing such a sin would diminish his favor with God.

PRAYER

God, I come to you humbly asking for you to cultivate in me a heart to defeat temptation. In my marriage, there will be temptations of all kinds. Temptation often stems from a desire within my heart or can start with a simple thought. Teach me how to overcome the thoughts of temptation and not ignore it. Temptation in and of itself is not a sin, it is the choices we make after the temptation that opens the door to sin. When a thought of temptation comes, I pray that I will resist it, and seek you for refuge. God, I pray that you send me a spiritual prayer partner that I can confide in, a husband that is constantly praying against any temptation that may come our way. I declare that we are protected from head to toe physically and spiritually. Let us use these tools and be ready to win the war against temptation because we have the armor of God within us.

In Jesus name, Amen

Investment Account

"How then could I do such a wicked thing and sin against God."
Genesis 39:9

Read this verse and connect how you view temptation, and what strategy can you implement to overcome temptation in your marriage. For me, I am trying to protect my mind and thoughts by not fantasizing about certain situations. I guard my heart by thinking about the greater things that God has in store for me and how I can ruin it if I give in to temporary satisfaction.

Bonds:

____

____

____

Stocks:

____

____

____

____

____

SIXTEEN
GOLIATH OF LUST

Within this devotional I have mentioned the apostle Paul quite a few times because he has great insight on how to overcome our sinful desires and be transformed with the Spirit of Jesus Christ living within us. Apostle Paul went into detail about breaking free from the bondage of lust, fleshly desires and how to strengthen your spirit man. Before we defeat lust, we must understand what it is. Lust starts with a thought in your mind that you later act on. When you see someone attractive that is normal. However, lust begins when you intentionally start to fantasize and daydream about intimate things that you can do with that person. Lust is dwelling on someone's physical attraction and using it for your own sexual arousal. So, how do you overcome lust? Great question! Apostle Paul also talks about how your mindset should shift to that of what the spirit desires. Now, when you go into battle with the Goliath of lust you must change your mind and take captive of your thoughts. It is easier said than done, but just take a second to think about God, his love and compassion for us... See you can quickly shift your thinking, so in the same way, you can meditate on the goodness of God instead of being succumbed to lust lustful thoughts.

Owei, today I am praying against the chains of lust. They no longer have a stronghold over my life. My lustful desires started from others' wickedness as a child or when I was introduced to sexual behaviors. I recognize the root, and fast and pray that you help me to become free. If my husband struggles with lust, I ask that it is long gone before our marriage. Anything that may have happened to him as a child, obsession with pornography, sex, and masturbation, I declare that he is set free. I pray that I nor my husband have wondering eyes, indulge in self-gratification, daydream, or fantasize about others. I also pray that I am set free from lustful dreams. I declare that we will use sex in the way it was intended by God.

In Jesus name, Amen

Investment Account

"Those who live according to the flesh have their minds set on what the flesh desires; but those who live in accordance with the spirit have their minds set on what the Spirit desires." Romans 8:5

Read this verse and contemplate some 'quick thoughts' that you can shift your mind to if you are struggling with lust. Then think about some ways that you can implement to protect yourself from sexual temptation or lust. For me, my quick thought is from scripture reminding me if I commit lust in my eyes, I have already committed adultery in my heart (Mat 5:28).

Bonds:

____

____

____

Stocks:

____

____

____

SEVENTEEN

SAY IT WITH ME, *"BOUNDARIES"*

♡

Let me introduce the bold Sista Ms. Vashti. No one exalts her because of the outcome of a decision she made but let us break it down. King Xerxes was married to Vashti before Esther. The King hosted an event and invited other kings and officials to celebrate with him for a week. On the seventh day he called for his Queen Vashti to wear her crown and to show her beauty to the King's attendants. Vashti heard this and told her servant in today's lingo "Boy bye." Seriously, Vashti refused to do what the King requested and that was a big no no because women were not allowed to go against their husband's request much less the King's. Such an act was disrespectful to the King, and he had to make an example out of her so the other women would not follow suit. The King asked his officials what he should do, and they encouraged him to dethrone her and find a new Queen. This is what led to Queen Esther's crowning which was God's plan to save Israel. Although

Vashti's actions were done out of a heart of defiance, I am going to swing it another way just for this lesson. Do not be intimidated by Vashti boldness, because she set her boundaries no matter the consequences or the position. She obeyed her boundaries so much; she was willing to give up her crown and stick to who she was. The lesson here is not to be defiant but be confident to set boundaries in your life that honors God.

PRAYER

Father, I come to you today asking for the strength to set boundaries and to respect my husband. I pray that we set boundaries in the marriage that allow us to prioritize God, each other, and our children. We will spend quality time with each other and have designated time to unwind away from each other. Let us be open about our boundaries in our marriage and make them clear at the beginning of the relationship, so it can help us to better understand each other. If we have children, or they are already in the picture, we will make a schedule to make them feel just as important. I pray that we do not over-prioritize work, our children or each other. We ask God to guide us to have a balance. I know that having boundaries will keep us from being stressed and everyone feeling important and loved.

In Jesus name, Amen

Investment Account

"For the queen's conduct will become known to all the women, and so they will despise their husbands and say, 'King Xerxes commanded Queen Vashti to be brought before him, but she would not come."
Esther 1:17

Read this verse and write down an identity statement for yourself. Then write down some boundaries you can set to become that woman in the identity statement. My identity statement is, living out my purpose truthfully, boldly, and righteously. A boundary I have in place is to not let others shut me down, and do not allow the secular to overcome me.

Bonds:

____

____

Stocks:

____

____

____

EIGHTEEN
SACRED TIES

♡

If you were raised with your grandparents, then you will know that special song that they loved. *"Let's get it on"* by Marvin Gaye...but let us scratch the record for a second and talk about sex and intimacy in marriage. I am trying to say let us have "the talk" without making it awkward. God wants us to engage in physical intimacy with our SPOUSE. In fact, scripture shows us that it is a necessity, not a weapon or a reward. I repeat...when used the right way! Be mindful of the importance of intimacy with your spouse, have the knowledge of the power it holds and the self-control to use it in the right way.

PRAYER

God, today I pray about the sexual relationship with my husband. I pray that you give us the strength and courage to wait until marriage. If we dishonor you in any way, do not allow the enemy to flood us with self-condemn, shame, and guilt. In the case of a mistake or error, I pray that we will always find our way back to you. When we get married, I pray we can communicate about intimacy openly. Even as seasons change in our lives, I pray that we will keep our marriage and intimacy alive. Let our marriage glorify you and let us continue to honor and respect each other as our marriage is a gift from you.

In Jesus name, Amen

Investment Account

"Honor marriage and guard the sacredness of sexual intimacy between wife and husband. God draws a firm line against casual and illicit sex."
Hebrews 13:4 MSG

Read this verse and think about some ways that you can preserve intimacy in your marriage. How will you communicate openly about your sexual desires to your future husband when the time comes? Do not be afraid to have this conversation, welcome it! It is a vital part of a healthy marriage.

Bonds:

____

____

____

Stocks:

____

____

____

____

NINETEEN
ALLOWING HEADSHIP

As soon as women see the scripture *"Wives must accept the authority of your husbands"* (1 Peter 3:1) the first thing that comes to mind is who? me? Naw. But too many times that saying is given without accurate context, because it is the husbands job to lead the house and for a woman to respond with submission. Later in that chapter (1 Peter 3:7) it says, *"In the same way, you Husbands must give honor to your wives"*. So, I am going to leave you with some green flags that you should be looking for in your future husband. The first is making sure that your future husband is under the headship of God. As a wife, it will be easy to follow your husbands lead when you have confidence that he is following the way of Christ. Also, God knows him, and God knows you, so God will be able to guide him in the correct way to lead the family and it will not feel like a dictatorship. Secondly, your husband should love you just as much as Christ loved the church, he died for it. It will be easier to submit to your husband when you know he loves you so much that he would die for you! Third, your future husband should be protective of you and your children! He should be firm and confident in his leadership, knowing that when he says something it is for your safety. Now this one is my favorite.... sacrifice. As you sacrifice for your family, it will be matched by the sacrifice your husband is also making.

As we close, check for green flags in your future husband's moral and educational standards, he should always be instilling principles and knowledge in your household. Your husband should also be a provider. He should be doing everything in his willful power to give you and your family the necessities in life. I know this may be a lot to take in, but these green flags should be the initial thoughts before any man stand before you and make the claim that he is your future husband.

PRAYER

Abba, I thank you that my husband has all the green flags and so much more. I pray that he knows how to lead and be the head of our marriage and our children. I know from scripture how Christ loved the church, and the same is expected from my husband. Help me to be a submissive woman. Help me to be submissive to you so it is easy to submit to my husband's leadership. Allow me to place trust and assurance in my husband's headship. Most importantly, God, change my mind set on submission and help me to become more yielding to the role of a woman in marriage.

In Jesus name, Amen

Investment Account

"But I want you to realize that the head of every man is Christ, and the head of the woman is man, and the head of Christ is God."
1 Corinthians 11:3

Read this verse and think about how your posture in relation to your husband's headship. Write down some more green flags that you can look out for.

Bonds:

____

____

____

____

Stocks:

____

____

____

____

____

____

TWENTY

CORRECTION CONNECTION

♡

One day Jesus was invited into the house of a woman named Mary. No, not his mother Mary. To not cause any confusion, let us call her "Mo." Mo had a twin sister, Martha, who was distracted with her duties around the house. Mo decided, however, that if the Messiah is on Earth, she would sit at his feet, learn about him, and not get caught up with house duties like Martha. However, Martha was not having it and in my own words said 'Jesus, respectfully my sister needs to help me with my duties. I need you to back me up and say something to her.' Jesus took this moment to show Martha the things that are important. Jesus corrected Martha's attitude by commending Mo's reverence to him. In your marriage, it is important to note that what may be important to you may not be important to your husband. If correction is necessary on your part, it is important to correct your husband from a place of love and respect.

Jesus, sometimes correcting my spouse means stepping back and allowing you to work on his heart. I pray that my husband has a heart to be opened to correction. When we try to correct out of our own understanding it can sometimes come across as selfishness which may cause the other person to shut down or be defensive. Healthy correction can also come from being an example. Lord Jesus, you corrected your disciples many times by being an example. Your actions always showed the fruits of the spirit. Many times, you did not have to say anything to correct your disciples, even though you have the power to, instead you just displayed it. I come to you asking for a heart to not only correct my husband in love, but also a heart to receive correction in love.

In Jesus name, Amen

Investment Account

"You are worried and upset about many things, but few things are needed- or indeed only one."
Luke 10:41-42

Read this verse and address how you might approach correction in your marriage, and how you desire to be corrected by your husband. For me, I like to have my own space to think, pray, and find the best way to approach things. I would want my husband to correct me with honesty and a pure and genuine heart.

Bonds:

Stocks:

TWENTY-ONE
DOLLA DOLLA BILLS

♡

Now I know there is going to be a few independent women reading this book, a few hustlers as well, and all my women out their getting their own! Let me tell you sis, when you get married, you are going to have to share all that *"bread."* Gasp I know. Really though, finances are the number one reason couples do not get married or struggle in their marriage. In this devotion, I will share a story in Matthew about three servants who all got a bag (for those who may not know what a bag is, its money!).

The boss met with all three servants and left one servant five bags of gold, the other two bags of gold, and the third - one bag of gold. The first and second spent their time investing the money (how ironic, that is exactly what you are doing right now by waiting) and they earned double of what they were given. The third servant chose not to invest and went back with nothing.

He buried the bag until his boss returned. When the boss came back, he asked, 'how have you been spending my money?' The first two said they doubled it and the boss said, 'You have done well, and proven yourself to be my loyal and trustworthy servant. The third came up with a story and in my own words said "Boss, look I was afraid of you, so I hid your money and buried it." The boss said, 'You're an untrustworthy and lazy servant!'

In the same way you will have to trust your partner to share your hard-earned money as they will have to share theirs with you. Have conversations with your partner about each other's expectations of how you want to spend your money, saving habits, joint bank accounts, tithing, etc. You even need to have a conversation about, I am about to say a cuss word so excuse my language, CREDIT SCORE! Do not go into your marriage naive about financial stewardship or financial knowledge overall. You and your spouse work hard for your money, so work even harder to know each other's financial strengths and weaknesses to contribute to a happy fruitful marriage.

Father God, I ask that you guide my husband and I to cultivate a sound financial plan before and during our marriage. No matter if we think in our natural minds, that we do not have the finances to sustain a marriage, we know that if it is your will we can overcome and work through that challenge. Help us to learn financial literature and create wealth not only for ourselves but for our inheritance. Lord, I ask that there is a certain expectation around loyalty and trust between my husband's finances and mine. We know that money is not the root of all evil, but the love of money is the root of evil, so I ask in my marriage we do not prioritize the need for money over you Lord. Give enough to sustain us. Teach us how to enjoy money, use it to give back, provide for our family, and anything else that we may need to know on how to use money wisely. At the end of the day Lord, we know true riches of wealth come from you.

In Jesus name, Amen

Investment Account

"Commending his servant, the master replied, 'You have done well, and proven yourself to be my loyal and trustworthy servant. Because you have been a faithful steward to manage a small sum, now I will put you in charge of much, much, more."
Matthew 25:21 TPT

Read this story and think about how you can become a better financial steward before getting married. Write down some financial weaknesses that you may want to share with your future husband. For me, I can be a better financial steward by saving money. I always want to use the money right away and feel as if I must get whatever I want right now instead of having patience, taking that money, and saving it.

Bonds:

____

____

Stocks:

____

____

TWENTY-TWO

NANI'S HOUSEHOLD

♡

Note: What God is doing in my life is a continuation of what he was doing in generations before me, so this chapter is co-written by me and my Nani (because she does not like to be called grandma). I wanted to add a chapter about the importance of family and there is no better person to add a prayer and talk about family then the woman who raised me herself because as she always said, "as for me and my house, we will serve the Lord."

Sarah, Hagar, and Abraham in Genesis are the perfect example of a blended family. Sarah, Abraham's wife, was unable to conceive so she came up with the idea of having their servant Hagar lay with Abraham. Sarah is way better than me because of the amount of self-control that this plan would require! Hagar ended up having a son named Ishmael and turns out... Sarah did not have as much self-control as she thought. She started to despise Hagar and her fertile womb. Sarah got extra petty and put Hagar AND Ishmael out of the "casa" because jealousy got the best of her.

God did not leave Hagar by herself because he sent an Angel to meet her in the wilderness and the angel relayed a promise from God about her son Ishmael. Sarah did end up pregnant with a son named Isaac, who was the original promise from God. However, we learn from this story that a blended family may not be easy to accept. We can learn from Sarah's mistakes and encourage the idea of building a family honorable to God no matter the circumstance. If this is your experience, take on the task with joy.

PRAYER

Beer-Lahai-Roi is what Hagar called you Lord when she was crying out to you, and you answered her. She called you 'Beer-Lahai-Roi" the 'well of the Living One who sees me.' Lord, I come to you crying out on behalf of my family asking that you cover us and protect us. Please give my family the strength every day to not conform to world's standards. As parents, you have given us headship over our children that we would lead and guide them according to your WORD. Allow my family to be an example for other blended families. I pray for the overall relationship between my husband's family and mine. I ask for a thriving and loving relationship with my mother-in-law, all my in-laws and vice versa. I ask that when our families combine it is a powerful force.

Strongholds, jealousy, shame, and anger will not destroy or disturb the merging of our families. I pray that my husband to have a good relationship with my parents and he can connect with them in a special way. I pray you use our marriage to break generational curses and be a pillar in our family for what a God-centered, God-ordained union is supposed to look like. I ask you to help us to love each family member for their unique pers. Teach us what it means to truly be a family.

In Jesus name, Amen

Investment Account

"Then the angel of the Lord told her, "go back to your mistress and submit to her." The angel added, "I will increase your descendants so much that they will be too numerous to count." Genesis 16:9-10

Read this verse and write down the relationship you want to have with your future husband's family. Then write how the people around you have helped build your version of a kingdom "family."

Bonds:

____

____

____

____

Stocks:

____

____

____

____

TWENTY-THREE
CREATING COMMUNITY

♡

Jesus had a sleepover on a mountain, but the only people at the sleepover were him and God. Jesus being the 'golden child' prayed to his Father, and they spent some Father and son time. When the morning came, he went out and chose his disciples. I do not know about you, but Jesus making friends seemed a little too easy. If the younger me knew all I had to do was pray before I chose friends, I would have done that! The important thing is how serious he was about choosing his disciples. There is no telling what Jesus' prayed on the mountain or if he even prayed for God to lead him to his disciples. The lesson here is to seek the Lord regarding your selection of friends, community, and those you choose to walk closely beside you.

Lord, bless me and my husband with a community that is centered around you. I ask you that anyone that we spend time for work or leisure is aligned with your purpose for our lives. I pray that my husband will have a powerful group of men who he can confide in and open his heart to. I ask the same for me that you surround me with prayer warriors, women who can support me on my journey. I pray that our friends have pure intentions and kind hearts in our lives. I pray for discernment when it comes to having friends with the opposite-sex. I also ask that you take jealousy, anger, and any over-friendly spirit out of the heart of me and my husband. Overall, I come to you with the same heart posture as Jesus when he was on the mountain praying to you God.

In Jesus name, Amen

Investment Account

"One of those days Jesus went out to a mountainside to pray and spent the night praying to God. When morning came, he called his disciples to him and chose twelve of them, whom he also designated apostles"
Luke 6:12-13

Read this verse and write down some ways you and your future husband can be intentional within who is in community and people who you call friends.

Bonds:

____

____

____

____

Stocks:

____

____

____

____

BONUS

MIRCALES ON MIRCALES

♡

God, today I pray for blessings and miracles in my marriage. I pray that you bless us with knowledge, understanding, and wisdom regarding our covenant, and our purpose. God, I pray that you bless everything we touch and have together. From houses, cars, finances, intimacy, future or current children, peace, love, honesty, and humility. Everything God. If we think that we cannot overcome something as a couple, I pray that you will strengthen and equip us. Our pleasure in life is to serve you with a yielded heart.

SPRITUAL RETURN

♡

In the introduction I mentioned getting spiritual returns for investing in your spiritual stocks and bonds. After you have invested for 23 days, reflect, and write down your answered prayers and the areas that you were strengthened.